Word of mouth

John Stuart

Oversteps Books

First published in 2009 by   Oversteps Books Ltd
                                6 Halwell House
                                South Pool
                                Nr Kingsbridge
                                Devon
                                TQ7 2RX
                                UK

www.overstepsbooks.com

Oversteps Books acknowledges with thanks the financial assistance of Arts Council England, South West

Copyright © 2009 John Stuart
ISBN 978-1-906856-07-6

All rights reserved. No part of this book may be reproduced, stored in a retrieval system, or transmitted in any form, or by any means, electronic, mechanical, photocopying, recording or otherwise, or translated into any language, without prior written permission from Oversteps Books, except by a reviewer who may quote brief passages in a review.

The right of John Stuart to be identified as the author of this work has been asserted by him in accordance with the Copyright, Designs and Patents Act 1988.

Printed in Great Britain by imprint digital, Devon

Acknowledgements

Bronzes in the park was published in Lancaster Litfest Publications *Poems 25 – Literary Oxygen*, and shared the joint prize for 2002; and *Intruder*, under its previous title *The swallow*, was published in *The Somerset Reviewer*.

Front cover: Conversation piece by Charles Bray (1999) by kind permission of Artizana

... συνδυάζουσα τές μέρες.[1]

thanks, Sally, Julie, Ros, Meg and Raymond

---

[1] C P Cavafy: '...blending the days.'

Contents

Seasons	1
After school	2
Harvest watch	3
Don't go far	4
Barn dance	5
Litany	6
Runaway	7
Aspirations	8
Wandering albatross	9
King and queen	10
Martins	11
Buzzard	12
Bronzes in the park	13
Stormy petrel	14
Intruder	15
Workshop task	16
Boys	17
Word of mouth	18
Mind and matter	19
Between Paulin and Pinter	20
The perfect wood 1, 2, 3	21
Rugby practice 1, 2, 3	24
The Otterhead lakes 1 to 7	27
Stranger at the door	34
Taking leave	35
Brighton	36
On the promenade	37
Son	38
The old shed 1, 2	39
Something and chips	41
At the other side of the bed	42
Our house	43
To hide	44
Getting there 1 to 5	45
Two poems towards a sequence about Eurydice 1, 2	50
Arriving at the crematorium	52
Seascape with boats	53

Seasons

In this valley which each year marks
a season with its own taxonomy
rotating with the crop, just one steadfast hand
on his powered steed ploughs, harrows, sows,

sprays, harvests and stores. Like a genie
from his own sandwich box. He has no need
for his father's strong arms and legs,
only a good eye and steady hands. Alone

in the great field on his comfy seat,
mobbed by gulls and crows as the sun climbs
and falls, as the clouds bunch or fly, wind
or still air round his sealed cabin,

rain shot on his roof or the dead heat
across his shoulders. It's a shifting world.
And when he takes his path back to the farm
leaving his beast to the watch until morning

there is nothing to give the cooling earth.
Only the sad paper which is no sacrifice
sits in his back pocket, folded and out of sight
to set him ready for tomorrow.

After school

A comfort after school is to walk
through the village. Red brick against cold flint
and a grey stone church behind a screen
of yews. The stream is straighter than people
and bounces under the bridge; the chestnut tree keeps
more promises and waves across the road.

And still, nothing is doing. Old Mrs Smith
will meet young Mrs Webb in the square;
Mr Mac may be late again with the van.
The village is tired and slow. It has slept late
like a dear old aunt and has come to
not sure of the day. The bus will come
round the corner eventually to pant
at the pump and throw heat in the faces
of standers and starers. Even in snow.

A comfort after school is to walk
through the village, pause at the brick
and the stone, count the winds in the trees.
Mothers are there at the shop door
and talk as they wait for us behind the backs
of those who are yet to come.

Harvest watch

He stands in deep shadow while the sun grinds
the day off on its stone. The gun stock warm
on his arm, hot boots tight to his feet, sweat
beads in his eyes, he has stood a full slow,
torpid watch and waits for the midday mark.

You will not see him unless the husky *bam!*
of his twelve bore makes you look for movement;
and a few heads may turn, leading your eye.
A figure may bend in the black shadows
as his dog fetches and lies still again

at his heel. Then they will flicker and fade
under the mottled light at the field's edge.
If there had to be gods of the harvest,
talismans of childhood, and there were –
oh, yes, there were – it would be the watching men.

Men trusted with guns. But he does not see himself
in the role of god. By his own secular measure,
blinking and staring, shifting his weight, loosening
his arms, stifling his yawns, he's after rabbits
and that's all it is, watching as the field

is shaved of sanctuary. Let the boys ape
the rhythm of his gun, the smooth ease
of its snap, lock and glide to the shoulder;
the kick of its recoil. Let them laugh,
as their eyes lust for his metal monster.

A man should not be turned by admiration. ...
But when his son has come to the field's edge,
he finds the majesty in a straight back
and high head, wants the boy's eyes to pay
unmistaken homage to his dark shape.

Don't go far

You will always worry when he goes missing
but even the fox respects a boy
who needs to whip thistles or pull bark

from a tree. On his wandering trail,
he may kick an adder into the brush
or his heart may stop at a tussle of wind.

Bees may draw him into a wood
of elephants and tigers though you said
Don't go far to the tousled back of his head.

In the deep arctic he may fight bears,
lunge with his spear through the ice or dive,
in a breath, through the cold silence. Deep, deep

with the mermen and naked breasted maids.
And the vultures on their daily circuit
may hear your voice as you call him home.

Barn dance

Here is the iron barn: corrugated roof
and hanging rope frayed and knotted,
swung by the light breeze. It has no sides
and all its good red legs in their four pairs
are exposed. And the honey coloured bales,
a light bright honey. The shouts
of children reverberate. These are not
simple echoes but a challenge, a call
of your bluff musty, dusty old barn.

Get your legs dancing to their jumping beat
and tumbling games! Swing that rope and shout
along as though you know the words! Dig deep
in your honey bales for their cosy houses,
whispered secrets and giggling kisses.

Litany

By the silent river and its dark shine
under the bare sun; by the meadow's ripe

grasses and breeze that blew a flimsy mob
of travellers about its flowers; by the hub

that was an elm, I recall, and so tall,
so visible in all directions; by more

than we could count of nettle and thistle
on bare-legged walks and the bramble's hostile

thorns; by the cattle crowd on their quiet hill
as they pulled at the grass and ramblers *watched it*

hiking over the fields; by the barbed wire
fence, the stile and the five-barred gate I swore

I'd jump one of these days and on the roadway,
winding down into the village where sane

valley feet trod; by the church yews that stood
now out of their time and no longer stirred

their worshippers; by all these, we kept close
and made our quiet way all on our own.

Runaway

for Lawrence

In the autumn of his runaway year,
as the headlights picked up a dance of leaves
across the road works and chicane, he saw
a familiar sign that said: No through road.

And wind hissed through the thin gap at the top
of the driver's window. He tried to ignore
its constant complaint. 'If', the noise said, '*If!!*'
And it seemed, down in the running stream
at the carriageway's edge, in the blushing stream,
there was more than a liquid black snake.

But it was too dark. And it was too sudden.
'When the warm weather comes and the light nights',
he promised when we last spoke, 'I will have
more time to dispose on the old places.
In this weather, I must first think of home.'
And the wind cooed on through the open door.

Aspirations

Out in the field and quiet, they graze
and he is walking not with a crook handled stick
but a stave and its music swirls through the grass,
catches his step and his tight legs,

runs through his open shirt. He calls
but the day he wants is too short for these ladies,
too filled with his dull prospectus and they
sink lifted heads back into the spring tang.

If you need the truth, the rub of his song
is too easy and too blear. He will have to herd
his tiresome beauties, to make the warm sweat

of their rumps steam and drive them to the yard
if he wants them home. He lifts his tangled knees
and through the whistling heat trudges after them.

Wandering albatross

There are wild days when waves slash the air howling
and white dancers stretch for a passing chance
to drown something, when the broad troughs heave unhinged
and plunge away as though to graze the seabed
with their hungry scoops – while he rides thoughtlessly

over his spitting gradients, tends
his roaring garden, dips into his tombola for a fish;
or there are scorched weeks in the bare heat
when rising air is the only movement out to sea,
and the gasping glitter shifts and wriggles

searching out a comfortable reflection
in the glassy depths – but he skims the hidden lift of his great plain,
grooms himself in his scaly mirror,
adjusts the sun for the next leg and glides
to the horizon along his open corridor;

and across the wakes which work the seasons
each in its own way, each at its brief
position in the constellations, each
sweating and straining for the final tonne,
he flies to his rendezvous on the high cliffs of the south.

King and queen

You can't expect to see them kiss.
Their austerity comes from the sculptor's
hands and the tears they shed, from the sky.
I feel their languid arrogance
and see the sharpness in their eyes.

They lack a great hall and a voice
to make decrees but they have trapped
me in their whims and I am minded
to comply. Today their court is me alone.
I feel they will accept my service
as I touch my brow. And if they were to wish
to move an army or the tax man
from his bed, this courtier's and a royal
unblinking eye need only meet
and off at speed the messengers will ride.

I like the thought of me (in jeans and fleece)
to act the chamberlain and bow
then click my fingers, make the mechanism stir.
And they will sit correct and decorous
and easy in their roles, deferring joy
or fading hope until I tell them: yes,
the deed is done. Your power has been conserved.

Martins

As the weather warmed the day would come
when the air exploded with twittering
and excited martins. I checked my book:

white eggs as small as peas; mud nests
under country eaves; black suited, white shirted.
There were hundreds of them. And they would make

the spring from mud and spit, turn back the clouds
and inspect everything. Housekeepers,
busy tenders of the sky, agile little spitfires.

I could have simply flown away by looking
at them! *They come from Africa*
my mother said, *and bring good luck.*

When I told the gang, we stood in the lane,
outstretched for any luck they might gob
at us or in the puddles at our feet.

Buzzard

She may have had prey on her mind swooping
round across the hedge over my shoulder.
Or was she heavy, weighed down already
with a dead or struggling weight? If I had known

and could have watched her coming
I would have marvelled at her insolence or gasped
at her parabola but I was flat surprised

and left with just the scaling
of her back, the hunched wings that vanished
over brambles and down the hill. I looked

as far as I could. She did not appear
at the valley floor. As I lifted the fork
again and turned it round, I had a sense
of her turning for home in strong, slow time.

Bronzes in the park

They have no eyes and have no wish to look
though they seem to know movement and follow closely
the crowd of turning heads and comfortable arms
too busy to embrace them. I can stand quietly and feel a flow

which might ghost the steps walked round them,
but there are no blades of grass between their toes
and the park air whispers and whistles
round their familiar curves and corners.

They are burnished to the hard and wilful shine
for an outdoor meeting, though they cannot know
why so many come and might only feel
the cool sense of a shadow slipping through the air

and not know how to capture it. But when the crowd
has left the park, they may like to know
what has drawn *you* here so often and why echoes
ring through them at the touch of a perambulant hand.

Perhaps when you come again, they'll pretend to be alerted
as my stumbling footsteps hurry down the path
and entice their imprint from your eyes to reflect on
in the black hollows that may be their hearts.

Stormy petrel

In that tense roar on deck,
        there has to be music.
    It barges into all my secret
                places. And it keeps
my pulse awake as I stand where the wind
    has stretched and pleated the waves.
            The frantic rolls crash deafening
over the ship's hull.

            It is rowdy music. In-your-face,
        horny and hard
    and searches through my clothes
            for ecstasy, roughs me up when it finds
                  only shrinking flesh. Nothing
can be heard against it and
        the brash scrolling waves
push and pound under its treading pressure.

        I scan for the horizon. Music
      like this has a thundering
beat and I have no wings
                to fly the whipped and stinging
        waves,
    no webs to dabble in the cold
pleats and heaving rolls. I turn
          to cantilever over the rail,
to find a line in the grey wheals of the sky.

           There is black like notation
              scudding and whistling tunelessly
                  across the grey. Flak spray beating
              at my face to blast off
      the expression. I could be flayed
            and churned to bone and paste,
    lose my words, my witnesses heaving
                and smashed by the rolling
            waves.

Intruder
Powderham Castle, Exeter

It was hot. Hunters for insects were in the air,
whirling round the castle and the grounds –
above the human swirl which passed into the castle

and no doubt sounded to the hurtling birds
like mammoth beings trumpeting their deep greetings,
bellowing their slow laughs. Ponderous beasts

sucked up by the immortal rock. When a swallow
chased some small thing into the conference room
and its darkness sensors clicked in and its flight

geometry flicked to *confined space*, our meeting stopped
as though it had flown in to find us and make
an announcement. But it searched the walls, the space

in which we had confined ourselves – and,
without a false beat, left by the open window
through which it had come. We cheered its bold departure.

Not for the bird that was focussed on escape.
For our leaping hope as it swept out into the air;
for the sense of the marvellous we hold in ourselves.

Workshop task

The challenge was to choose an animal
to represent me. I wanted to take
an antlered stag. Not as a silk motif
or badge but standing on a crag tasting
the autumn's fickle air. He was a brute
and would come down among the herds, hard flame
to the soft rain that drenched the bare valley.

Was it truly sound for someone like me
with my reasons for staying put at home
to lay claim to this rough beast? Oh, I took
the discretion to be bold! His strong line
above the ordinary, his symmetry
of tines, his ruthless eye. – I always will
protest he was king of those mountains.

Boys

A simple ruse draws
the Caped Crusaders into the net
and escape seems impossible. Yet
they fight with skill, loop
the net over and in a flash
capture their captors.

They are acclaimed and full
of exaltation but they return exhausted
to their other life and their tiresome
daily necessities. For heroes
there is no fulfilment
like the flow of pursuit
and the whip of retribution.

To pull off the mask,
to hang up the cape, to disguise
themselves each day. These
are the nets with no escape
which have trapped them
as ten years old once more
and impatiently
incognito.

Word of mouth

I began to wonder how it would be
if I were photographed nude. A simple,
full frontal portrait to show I can be
as cheerful and unashamed as you get

through someone else's eyes. And I wondered
what people would say if I blew it up
to A3 size, framed it, let my image
display in the hallway over the years

his proclamation for our visitors.
I'd keep myself out of that, let him speak
for himself. I'd have made him a chance, though,
to be carried abroad on the loose tongues:

to be requested for performances,
give his autograph in the local shops,
take online orders for reproductions ...
and then slip me something for my trouble.

Mind and matter

Nightmare: strap hanging in a sweaty
squeeze of chests and elbows. Remember
the work of days and days braced
between your knees as someone's petty order
digs at your lower back? Remember

counting the stations? trying to leave?
Mind the gap! Mind the crowds of pushers
getting on. Mind the caps of peddlers
and their guilt music; the howling gales
of unsatisfied trains. Would the eyes not see

that you're really not there? Not really there!
Keep hold. Keep going, escalator!
It's the rush hour and you're far too late
for it now. You missed your rightful station; can't
get out 'til the end of the Yellow Line.

Between Paulin and Pinter

for Meg Peacocke

She comes and sits in the crowd I have
on the third shelf down and seems to fit.

She comes by special accord, I mean.
I shoved Paulin there earlier. He

annoyed me enough to bring him in;
but Pinter came with a friend one day

and has made himself redoubtable.
I don't want to change or to cram them

out of sight in a cupboard upstairs.
They make a good noise on my broad shelves,

and I wouldn't want to say who's best.
Meg came, sat between and unsettled

them, brought the encounter to a pitch
of fevered enlightenment because,

just like a woman, she's occupied
the only place to be: in between.

The perfect wood

1 Child hero

I want to feel like a woodpecker and drum
two fingers on the table hard to make
them wild and raw; and like a hawk twist

arms outstretched between sticks in the garden
as I search for food; in the badger sett
of my blanket camp snuffle with my mate,

my young and protect them from the claws
and teeth of dogs. I want to know every blue tit's nest,
every fox path and hideaway, to befriend

the hedgehogs, be wiser than the old owl
(who'll indulge my pretence) and help deny
men their booty. And as we all meet,

a jay will interpret from my wrist
with cheerful disrespect and then steal for me
all I could need for life in the greenlit wood.

2 Pheasant wood

On this bare spring day which warms our backs
but whips up a chill ploughfield wind,
the wood's meagre shelter spreads its blue welcome
and claps its branches at brigades of starlings
foraging in the field. Before the nettle curtain rises

and hides the old green stile, the way past the barbs
clambers over its slippery planks
to merge in a few steps with the sparse tangle.
In no more than a blink, we are gone from sight
and mind less that the sun which can't tell dark

from dark squints through the branches
than that the snap of undergrowth
marks out the line for the gamekeeper
whose only sound's like a tree's indignant sigh
but he can follow careless silence to its den.

3 Pathway to paradise

In the wood, we learn that paths are not set
except by walking on them. We have to look
for the compacted line over a bare ridge,
the foot-marked hollow winding over soft ground,

a scuffed track that many soles have pressed
and made infertile. Like travellers, follow
the clues not hidden by the trees. For where they can,
the young, ambitious saplings fill a clearing

or push a dry carcass to block a narrow file.
Then, when as good fellows we come, we stand lost
and for a second perhaps in the shade
half listen to their slowly breathed complaint,

though we cannot share their light and the wood
has stripped the laughter from our games. Our camp,
in that perfect spot hidden from the farm's many eyes,
is turned into a frightening paradise as we play.

Rugby practice

for Pete, who has always loved rugby

1 In the changing room

Today is cold. Hear the voices
warm our teenage spirits. The room

is bursting with our noise as though
it's really not manly to change

in silence. We stop for the *few words*
from the coach, and turn our heads

to a listening angle though
the concrete booms and no-one need

who does not wish to hear. Each bench
repeats its version of his story

and we all go out in the cold.
That sorts the hawks from the chickens! –

And you who love your boots gather
for the warmth of enlightenment

while we at the back are shuffling
in our cold silent comedy.

2 *On the field*

The drifts of fog are spreading out
across the Home Meadow blurring

the uprights and fading the grass.
The teams fan out to their places.

It's the standard coarse mixture
of partisans and policemen,

few of whom play just for playing.
But we are unknown quantities

and lazy sods that need watching.
We make the Honour of the School

turn on the pride of the bully boys.
And losers like us can make

such a balls of your game plan
that you'd elbow us away

if it weren't for the eagle eyes
or your own butterfly fingers.

3 *After the game*

We bring the sharp cold from outside,
clatter on the concrete floor slab

and separate, pure sheep and goat,
back to our clothes, bags and benches.

The door slams closed. The room steams up,
all strip and mud, hot breath and sweat. –

And all our bodies to shower
and soap. We make a queue, less those

who *forgot their towel* and slip
away to catch the early bus.

The rest dress and go as we can
while you gnaw the bones of the game,

clean and very casually late,
still naked. Under the lights outside

the rest of the school has gone home
and the fog is slowly lifting.

The Otterhead lakes

for the poets Chrissy Banks, Genista Lewes, Julie Sampson and Anthony Watts who walked with me and also wrote poems

Where shall we walk? I asked, not knowing where to find the picturesque or the beautiful round here and not wanting the task of deciding. *The Otterhead Lakes*, they all agreed. So that's where we went, though we met at The Greyhound in Staple Fitzpaine, which I knew and could find on my own.

1 The Greyhound

It's on a narrow English road,
which is full of curves and sightless corners,
sudden hills and narrow valleys
that modern cars take at a breeze.

And they shoot the corners too fast –
are they racing the weather? –
Or does the radio's music trap the swing
of wheel and pedals with its wicked beat?

I'm driving down to The Greyhound, then,
to rendezvous in its green hollow, to walk
this very plain Saturday as it gathers in
the cool of its wits and works on its clouds.

I park near the wall of the pub.
The grey, white and blue-grey stone warms
the deepening light that threatens rain.
More than a few spots.

2 A lift to the Otterhead car park

                    The all important question
for those invited to a seat in the back
at the navigator's calm insistence:
I'm navigating and his tight possession
of the map and the undoubted need
for three to go in the back is:
                    who goes in the middle?
To make it worse the car's a three door hatchback.
It makes you bow a second time
to the inevitable and put your back at risk
of mockery smeared on the door jamb.
                So who will volunteer?
Not me, I never do and no-one openly asks;
no eyes hit mine, so when the driver says
                "Shall we get off, then?"
one of the others gives in.

3 The upper lake

This was once a fancy place.
There were lawns for summer parties
round a big house which has gone now,

dissolved like a monastery. A few bricks or blocks
may be left but those, if you could find them,
would give no clue what they had stood for.

All we see now is grass where the house
used to light up the night and send its scratchy music
through the soft, damp air. Deep, uncut grass

which ripples from the lake to the wooded slope
by the road. You can walk right past
without a sense of the human task

to own and to enclose spaces. The lake,
the only focus for the eye now, lies,
like all still water left to its devices,

murky and green in its basin. It is free now
from all those traumas –
boats, fishing lines, swimmers –

that cut and churned it. It can abandon
its man-made past, pretend to an older
style of existence. Go wild ...

while we move on and on, seemingly,
and keep ourselves to the path that remains
for want of a better way to go.

4 The lower lake

We encountered three dogs,
their owner, a fisherman
and several species near the jetty
of wild plants Tony knew the names of.

And saw evidence of fish: blips on the water
made bright expanding rings
that skimmed across the lake.

Out in the deep, I saw them: fish
broke the surface for flies and beetles caught
by the tension. Blip! on the water

and a bright expanding ring ...

The others talked of scrophularia
and hemlock water dropwort;
pointed out to me the spotted orchid.

But my eyes were drawn to the water;
my spirit felt the tug of freedom.

5 The road to Churchinford

I have a metaphor of different appetites
to give a flavour of the walk: two gentlemen

were hungry, eating up the yards;
three ladies were not, and lightly nibbled at them

on our way to Churchinford. We, up ahead,
congratulated them, back there

for probing the hedgerow and, we imagined,
dissecting stems of inspiration: talk

and you feed images to your tingling fingers;
walk on and the waiting poem bubbles out.

We had each stepped out for his own purpose. –
Not admiration of roadside flowers

or the trees that sheltered us when it rained.
Not even for the wind on our cheeks

or the joy of the switchback road.
We went stride for stride, greedily marching

'til the first house rose from the earth ...
and we stopped to let the others catch us.

6 The field of bullocks

The bullocks gazed at us
with extreme fascination.
Walking fence posts,
their amazement seemed to convey,
were new in their experience.

They all crowded round and watched
while one brave soul approached
... and bounded off
with a laughing kick of his heels
when threatened by a shoo!

of hand and voice. Down the sloping field –
and back with childish leaps
to seek his answer once again.
What were these creatures?
Puffed with strange skins

and walking, most curious of all,
without buckets or feed bags or sticks or wire
or any apparent paraphernalia –
or dogs. Fence posts, then,
almost certainly. And moving fast.

7 The walk back to the car

We passed by dark trees along the road
and fields of sombre grasses.
We reflected pools and puddles
in our unsuspecting eyes
and spoke in hushed voices.

We met sparkling drips from branches and leaves.
They fell fast, as Galileo had predicted, and they fell on us.
Randomly.

        There was an evening sky
that might remind us of a sleepy child
that would not go to bed ...
but we ignored it
and spent the time talking
as companions have to talk
or seem unprofitable.

We talked –
about ourselves and poetry
and how we wondered,
in moments that melt with inactivity,
what confidence meant
to other people.

Stranger at the door

for Sally Issler

A stranger knocked at my door and asked
     my name. I thought it right to decline.
He looked the sort who might use his smile
     whatever his rights. Did I know mine?

I wondered at his motives and said
     the law would not insist on my name.
"I am not the law," he said and frowned,
     "I only knock. It is you who blame."

But why did he knock? I could not see
     the answer as we stood. He went
without shaking hands. I never saw
     him again. I asked my neighbour friend

what trust he put in the law. "I trust
     in my God; don't need the law. The life
I lead is right." I was frightened by
     his certainty. Both he and his wife

declared the stranger could claim no right
     to who I am. But still I must fear
for I am a stranger here myself
     and wish I could know why he came *here*.

Taking leave

i m Drummond Allison, poet (1921-43)

It was straight from the drifting spires
to be turned on a training spit
and made a foot soldier. Not good
but not unfair or unexpected.

And looked for, almost. To do one's bit. –
It brought a new persona: Officer,
though a sense of fraud might chuckle
up his spine before that first posting.

It was part of him, now, if all went well,
for the duration. As for leave,
he would choose to go home and made
no bones of the poetry of being

someone else. He felt real, of course
he bloody did, and it was good!
And the journey down to the port
with a rowdy mob of privates whistling

to the girls at every station. That
should keep him cheerful. Every soldier's
soldierly due before the lonely times
that had to be filled with something harder

like the letters that waited months
and no reply. That night, he'd join
the party and sing. Or throw himself
into some other chance occupation.

Or quietly read over, say, *Verity* ...
And next morning from the deck
of a crowded troop ship take his leave
as though he would be coming home.

*Allison was considered a promising poet while at Oxford
University. He died in the Italian Campaign at Monte Camino.
Verity is probably his most well known poem and one of his last.*

Brighton

Our mother brought us to the crowded beach
and put my little feet and little bottom
naked on the hot stones. We went down
near the water's reach and I played the game:

I dug out sand for my bucket to shape;
I kicked down the castles she said they built
for me. They trapped the sea in a lake
and I sat in the warmth of its shallows,
laughing when they pulled their acid faces.

I danced with the waves as they passed through them
leaving me between the blazing stones
and the heaving sea on my pale strip of gold.
I was King of the Castle, they had said,
but far from home and suddenly lonely.

On the promenade

When the weather is bad I just stand
set my eyes on the sea and the sand.

I love watching the waves and the greys
keep the wind in my face. I love spray.

I love wind though its freedom can hurt
like a blade when it leaps at the throat

with its salt and its cold and the lash
of its claws but I love it to thrash

round the deckchairs and beach vendor stalls
while my childhood's white horses still paw

at the beach and the crash of their hooves
makes the sand almost shriek as it rolls

down the shore and the slow ebb and flow
of the tide has me watching enthralled

all the breakers in sight all the greys
all the whites. There is no simple day

like a day on the shore with its wind
and bad weather and clouds in close hordes

and, whatever the weather, to stay
with my face to the sea and the sky
with my face to the wind and the sea.

Son

You should not imagine that
he's ever doing nothing. If you find him
thrown across the sofa, head
propped blankly on a hand and eyes
fixed on the sightless distance,

don't ask: he's occupied.
You may imagine that he's lost
in a desert without words,
a waste with no horizon
for the sun to climb. Life is a great jigsaw:

maybe he's lost a piece
and needs to work on where it dropped.
Or love is a well
down which he may have thrown
his last penny and is breathless

waiting for the splash. Or fortune
has an eye the size of the world
and he could be, he could just be
staring into the eye of fortune
trying not to blink.

The old shed

1 Then

I never used it
for the wicked things
boys do in sheds.

It wasn't the
transgressed in
sort of shed

though the door
shuddered erotically
when you pushed in

and out; and only
dad went there ... and only
sometimes. All the

tools hung down
rusting without oil
to excite them;

and the dust
flew in a rage
when it was stirred.

2 Now

There is no door
to barge through: it's on
the floor. And the floor

softens at my heel; and the roof
has shuffled half away
in the half lifetime,

slacked its remaining timbers
and surrendered.
And the scurry! Nails

under toolboxes, down holes;
screws and bolts dancing
to the edge. The gravitas!

augers, hammers, cutters,
bradawls, hacksaws,
knives, stakes, sticks ...

and all expecting
the hand of
resurrection.

Something and chips

His companion ordered
something and chips
and a glass to cheer the occasion.

But he knew the outcome already, knew he
could not drink to it. He took his knife,
cut his steak and kidney pie,

let the confusion, the heat,
the half-understood flavours drain out.
And he searched his cabbage

for the words to say no matter what
he was still the same fool
he always was. And the eyes watched

him across the table. You could see
they needed him to look up
from the islands on his plate.

He could feel the impossible
answer stuck half way
and swallowed hard.

At the other side of the bed

At the other side of the bed there are flowers
but here I am among cabbages and rhubarb
and the drops of rain slipping from their fleshy lips.

At the other side of the bed the perfume's sweet
but here I am surrounded by beans and lettuce
where the slugs have left their silver trails through the night.

At the other side of the bed there is nectar
but here I am among the chives and potatoes
to dig up the tubers before they rot away.

The best side of the bed is the one you lie on.
The soft earth and mulch and orderlies like roses,
sweet peas and honeysuckle which attract the bees
(with beetles hiding in their soft folds) and your eyes
waiting for the sun to shine now the rain has stopped.

Our house

It's our house, he said and didn't blink
or smile though red it was not and square
it was not and the tree was not there
but on the other side. Lovely, she said
in her perfect voice. Though it was odd,
she thought, had always thought it was odd
not wonderful what the child drew.

                                              And that's
my window, he said. It was green and barred
and shrunken high in the corner, smudged
by the finger which pointed. His hands were matt
with chalk; his cheeks rough with pale colours.
And the yellow sun was green where the blue sky
overlapped and the chimney smoke billowed.
Oh, she said, is that *your* window? Yes.

To hide .....

for Rita

.....I must creep
into that little place
where the air is close
and a dark hush
clicks to with the door.

I have to wait.

When I see your light
protesting at my feet,
hold my breath
as if it were the last place
you would ever look.

Keep down
punching laughter
that would snap at your heels.

Thumb tears I remember
from the pushchair
out of practised eyes

and keep closed
long nailed fists
desperate for noise.

Getting there

*for our granddaughter, Lily, who was christened on
31 July 2007 in Kandalos, Greece*

1 Somewhere over Europe

In the air, noise makes conversation troublesome
and the one reads while the other may watch the ground
scroll slowly by. Or read. And there are the puzzles
bought at the airport if we're really bored. We don't

generally talk. That way we keep our voices
for when we land. I have the window seat, daylight
and the jigsaw of Europe – or bits of it – dense
below me. No borders, anthems, colour coding.

Just patchwork. – And I quickly don't know where we are.
From the flat green of sparkling Holland, over cloud
in bright pockets, we scribe a line taut as it's cold

and we may appear, if you look straight up at us
and the passing silver of our plane, far too smug,
insisting we've found a great place for fun.

2 Coming to land at Athens Airport

We've come down Euvoia[2],
straight down the mainland side
and seen its fires, the smoke
staining its bright blue sea
for miles. And there has been
smoke down the Balkan spine

of parched valleys and black
mountains. From our cruise height,
the grey smudges stood out
as if they were the wind
itself, made visible
by its lack of magic: Rain.

And we with our floods
floundering at The Pale!
We have been looking down
on our tangled Europe
but at last we can see
Athens, its famous hill

made smooth and soft by sun
and haze. From here, we swing
down on the rush of air
losing that perspective,
losing the tireless drone
of an uneventful flight.

There were many forest fires across Greece in the heat wave and drought of 2007; while in England, there was widespread flooding owing to torrential rain.

---

[2] Pronounced Evia, an Aegean island close to the Greek mainland

3 Arriving in Patras

We are helpless, not speaking the language
and in the sun, not safe with our white skin.
The news is crackling with the forest fires

that spread with bounding ease across the roads.
And yellow 'copters dip down to the sea
then grumble overhead with bags of it

towards the line of flame. We saw from the car
as we arrived the pale flicker and ash
in the dinning light of the afternoon.

But it is deemed safe in a city house
and, three times trapped: by language, sun and fire,
we drink frappés and let the burning pass.

4 Shopping

We sit under the lemon tree and wait
for the sun to leave us by the western wall.
The canary sings in his high cage
and that emphatic voice makes the heat

of the courtyard easier to ignore. We shop
at dusk in crowds on unfamiliar streets;
the people we meet are shadows as we nod

and smile and shake hands to order. It feels
like Elysium lit by its own stars[3]
and restless and stark and ambiguous ...

But the eyes, bright fires bring back the senses:
of purpose, of place, of the crowd yielding.
We choose the things we need for the party,
to set the tone: not too light nor too hearty.

---

[3] Virgil, *The Aeneid 6.541*.

5 Kandalos

for Lily's other grandfather

And now we run the last, enticing leg
past blackened hills - and some are still in flame;
past ancient villages and plodding flocks
of unrelenting goats on the metalled road.

In the callous heat, the road curls round
the mountains' skirts and rolls over passes,
but we're air-conditioned cool and sail on
to the village in comfortable style.

And now to take its air: spartan and empty,
caught in the silent economics of change,
it is high up a mountain which plunges
to the valley like a hawk. Are there ghosts
in the orchard we're invited to enjoy?

There are *names* everywhere: in the water
of the stream, in the clang of the church bell,
in the scrawl on a barn. It beats the heart
to be here and have known nothing of them;
to look but not to see where they may have led.

And the dusty, stony track as we go
to the christening mumbles a liturgy
and the breeze cools the balloons in their dance
and there is more to come but I don't
understand what all those feet are singing.

Two poems towards a sequence about Eurydice

for Tzina

1 Eurydice
She had a wicked smile
and her black hair curled like a wolf
round her ripening face.

And she spoke to the boy,
made him wait by the stone path –
for her lightness warned his eyes –

and turned back with glistening conquest
on her cheeks. Did he touch her?
Did anyone see?

And the village watched as she went
with her friends past his house.
Heads were shaken. She would go too far.

She walked with a golden apple
sucked to her lips as if to bite.
It was Autumn and the harvest

brought from the hills farmers,
shepherds, cowmen to drink a glass
to her laughter while the boy sang

at her door. They went well together,
her laughter and his song,
like a spin of wool and the wheel.

2. The voice of Orpheus

He could sing like the softest breeze
He could sing like howling wind and rain
He could sing like the snow like the pale sun
Like the scorch of a dry summer day

Vast crowds would beg him to sing
They gathered in open fields to listen
Many would stand in the stark sun
Many more in the soft dark of night

He would sing of the mountain trails
He would sing of the valleys and rivers
He would sing of home and the pain of love
And of heroes in war and their fame

He had songs of desire for a better life
Of poor children of struggle of pain
He had songs of rich fools and old bridegrooms
Of the wise man who knows how to fail

There was hardly a song that he didn't know
There was never a note that was sour
And when he would sing no more the sound
Of his voice stayed with them hour after hour

He could sing like the softest breeze
He could sing like howling wind and rain
He could sing like the snow like the pale sun
Like the scorch of a dry summer day

Arriving at the crematorium

i m Russell 'Fish' Sage, 1912-2007, teacher of French

You come to the crematorium
knowing your suit is sombre and your face
composed. You drive smoothly through
to the low building, past trim lawns
and discreet beds of flowers and shrubs.

When you've parked the car, you take time
to sit and watch who goes past,
to compare them with the faces
you remember. None stirs up the music
of that era: no *Blue Suede Shoes*;
no *Peggy Sue*. You might at least
have hoped for one. But now, it's time
you went in, a good time to find
what you can say about the past.

And to meet the family
that saw him through while all
old pupils like yourself remember
is those fiery cameo roles he played
in *your* shows. You have to face
what you really came here for – you
had a bit part in his life, too.
        I'm glad.

Seascape with boats

Playa Honda, Lanzarote

Farther out there may be a beach but here
there is a lava scramble still shiny and,
from time to time, still washed by sparse waves
that hardly break. Further on as we walk
small white breakers float softly to the shoreline,
skip up the rocks and vanish in the dusk.

I can't think what to say that would not spoil
in the air so I am, dumb man that I am,
simply an arm to hold, a profiled face
to walk beside, a shirt you may yet admire.
The boats are resting in the shallow bay
not far ahead but I know what they want:

they have set themselves to captivate you
on the restaurant veranda; to beg
of me some kind of immortality
as the warm night closes in on our table.
It is a picturesque scene, we agree –
and we have to talk of something, don't we?

But they, meanwhile, sit silent and at ease,
winking on the blackened tide; lit softly
by the restaurant lights. Matt red, white, blue and black,
they've wilted into looser shapes now the sun,
somewhere over the island, sets in a blaze
we don't see, remote, splendid and unashamed.

Other books published by Oversteps

Anthologies: Company of Poets and Company of Four
David Grubb: An Alphabet of Light
Giles Goodland: Littoral
Alex Smith: Keyserling
Will Daunt: Running out of England
Patricia Bishop: Saving Dragons & Time's Doppelgänger
Christopher Cook: For and Against Nature
Jan Farquarson: No dammed tears
Charles Hadfield: The nothing we sink or swim in
Mandy Pannett: Bee Purple & Frost Hollow
Doris Hulme: Planted with stones
James Cole: From the Blue
Helen Kitson: Tesserae
Bill Headdon: Picardy.com
Avril Bruten: In the lost & found columns
Ross Cogan: Stalin's desk
Ann Kelley: Because we have reached that place
Marianne Larsen: A Common Language
Anne Lewis-Smith: Every seventh wave
Mary Maher: green darlings
Susan Taylor: The suspension of the moon
Simon Williams: Quirks
Genista Lewis: Cat's Cradle
Alwyn Marriage: Touching Earth
Miriam Darlington: Windfall
Anne Born & Glen Phillips: Singing Granites
A C Clarke: Messages of Change
Rebecca Gethin: River is the Plural of Rain
W H Petty: But someone liked them
Melanie Penycate: Feeding Humming Birds
Andrew Nightingale: The Big Wheel
Caroline Carver: Three Hares

www.overstepsbooks.com